Dedication

This children's book marks the dedication to my first grandchild, Jaeden. I decree and declare Numbers 6:24-26 over you, may the Lord bless you and keep you, may the Lord make His face shine upon you and be gracious unto you. May the Lord turn His face towards you and give you peace. Let wisdom and knowledge be the stability of your times and seasons. Be a good friend and may good friends find you.

DAVID AND JONATHAN WERE FRIENDS
WHO LOVED EACH OTHER.

DAVID MEANS 'BELOVED' OR 'FAVORITE'.
JONATHAN MEANS 'GIFT OF GOD'.

DAVID WAS THE YOUNGEST OF EIGHT
SONS BORN TO HIS FATHER JESSE.

DAVID AND HIS FAMILY
LIVED IN BETHLEHEM.

DAVID WAS A SHEPHERD WHO
TENDED HIS FATHER'S SHEEP.

DAVID WAS KNOWN FOR HIS COURAGE IN PROTECTING HIS FATHER'S SHEEP FROM A BEAR AND A LION.

DAVID WAS ALSO SKILLFUL AT PLAYING THE HARP AND WOULD PLAY FOR KING SAUL TO MAKE KING SAUL FEEL BETTER WHEN HE WAS SAD.

JONATHAN WAS THE SON
OF KING SAUL OF ISRAEL.

JONATHAN WAS VERY
KIND TO DAVID.

JONATHAN AND DAVID'S FRIENDSHIP GREW IN KING SAUL'S PALACE.

DAVID BECAME FAMOUS IN ISRAEL AFTER HE USED A SLING AND A STONE TO DEFEAT GOLIATH, WHO WAS AN ENEMY OF THE ISRAELITES.

THE WOMEN IN NEARBY
TOWNS CAME OUT TO
CELEBRATE AND PRAISED
DAVID MORE THAN THE KING.

JONATHAN'S FATHER ONCE HELD AFFECTION FOR DAVID, BUT HIS AFFECTION SHIFTED TO JEALOUSY BECAUSE OF DAVID'S POPULARITY WITH THE PEOPLE.

KING SAUL, JONATHAN'S FATHER,
KNEW THAT DAVID WOULD ONE
DAY BECOME THE KING OF ISRAEL
AND INHERIT HIS THRONE.

HE TRIED MANY TIMES TO
HURT DAVID AS A RESULT.

KING SAUL ALSO TRIED TO TURN
JONATHAN'S HEART AGAINST
DAVID...

...BUT KING SAUL DID NOT SUCCEED.

BOTH JONATHAN AND DAVID
WANTED TO DO GOD'S WILL.

WHEN JONATHAN LEARNED
THAT HIS FATHER WANTED TO
HURT DAVID, HE WARNED DAVID
OF KING SAUL'S PLAN.

JONATHAN DID NOT ALLOW
LOYALTY TO HIS FATHER TO BLIND
HIM FROM DOING WHAT HE KNEW
WAS RIGHT.

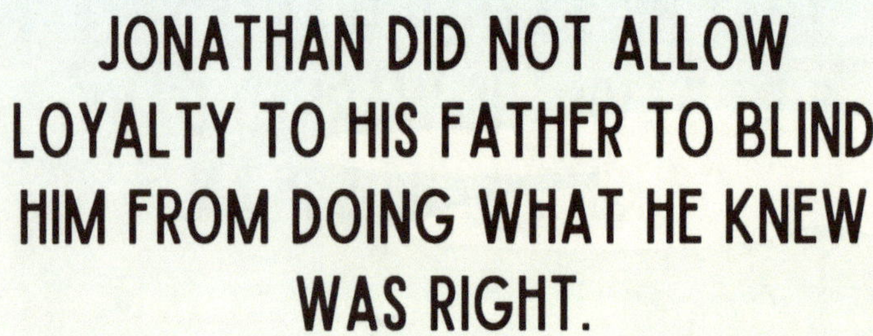

THEY WERE TRUE FRIENDS.

WHAT CAN WE LEARN FROM DAVID AND JONATHAN'S FRIENDSHIP?

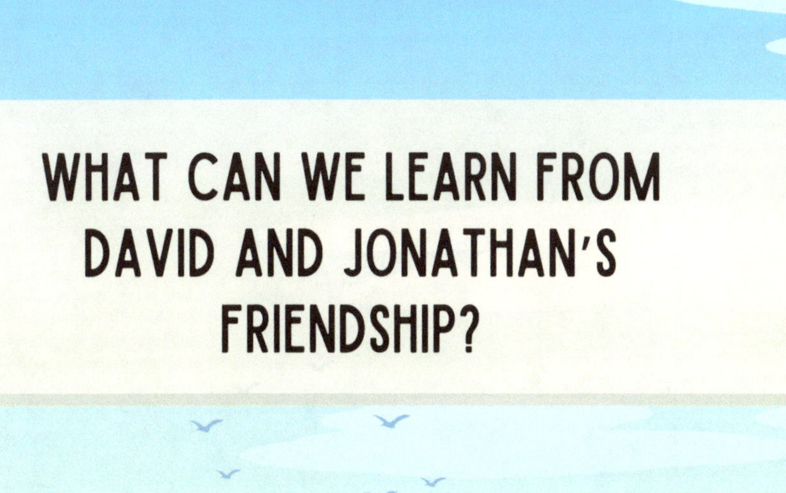

A TRUE FRIEND IS SOMEONE TO CELEBRATE. A TRUE FRIEND, LIKE JONATHAN, WILL ALWAYS SUPPORT YOU WHEN TIMES ARE GOOD AND WHEN TIMES ARE HARD.

A TRUE FRIEND WILL TELL YOU THE TRUTH EVEN WHEN IT HURTS.

A TRUE FRIEND DOES NOT TALK
BAD ABOUT YOU OR SPREAD
RUMORS BEHIND YOUR BACK.

A FAKE FRIEND OFTEN PRETENDS TO BE
ON YOUR SIDE BUT WILL ABANDON YOU
WHEN YOU ARE IN TROUBLE.

BE CAREFUL OF FAKE FRIENDS.
ASK GOD TO SHOW YOU WHO YOUR TRUE
FRIENDS ARE.

A TRUE FRIEND (LIKE DAVID) STICKS CLOSER THAN A BROTHER.

PROVERBS 18:24